MW01519513

The story of Moses in the bulrushes is found
in the Old Testament of the Bible,
in chapters I and II of Exodus.

The text of this book
has been prepared with reference to:
The Good News Bible (1994),
The New English Bible (1970),
The New Jerusalem Bible (1990),
The Revised Standard Version (1973).

Series editor: Jacqueline Vallon

*The publishers wish to thank
Geoffrey Marshall-Taylor, Educational Consultant,
for his kind help.*

ISBN 1 85103 269 X
© 1997, Gallimard Jeunesse
Illustrations coloured by Anne Gutman
English text © 1998, Moonlight Publishing Ltd
First published in the United Kingdom 1998
by Moonlight Publishing Ltd, 36 Stratford Road, London W8
Printed in Italy by Editoriale Libraria

Best Bible Stories

THE STORY
OF MOSES
IN THE BULRUSHES

Retold by Clare Best
Illustrated by Maurice Pommier

Moonlight Publishing

It was a long time since Jacob had left Canaan, where the Hebrew people lived. He had travelled to Egypt with his family: women, children and grandchildren, altogether about seventy-five people. They brought with them their animals and everything they owned, and settled in the Nile delta.

Jacob had come to live near his son
Joseph, who had risen to be the most
important person in Egypt, after
the Pharaoh. Joseph's wisdom and
planning had saved Egypt from
a terrible famine.

Many years passed.
Jacob's family, his
children and grand-
children, grew up
and in turn had their
own families. Egypt
was filled with
Hebrews. A new
Pharaoh, who had
not known Joseph,
became worried
that there were too
many Hebrews,
and that they were
too powerful.
He feared that in
a war they might
rise up and fight
him. He said to
his people,
"These Hebrews
could join forces
with the enemy
or even leave
our country."

"We must find some way to prevent their numbers from increasing even more," said the Pharaoh.

So the Egyptians put slave-drivers in charge of the Hebrews, and forced them to do back-breaking work. This was meant to crush their spirits.

The Hebrew slaves were made
to build two cities – Pithom and
Rameses – with grain stores for
the Pharaoh.

But the more harshly the Hebrews were treated, the more they grew in numbers, and spread out across the land.

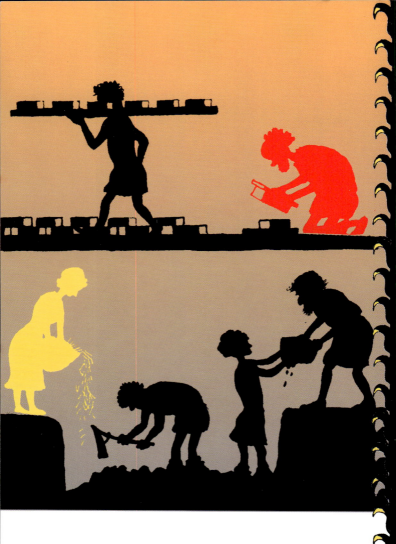

The Egyptians began to fear the
Hebrews, for it seemed that they were
everywhere.

The Egyptians treated the Hebrews
more and more cruelly, making their
lives miserable with hard work.
They gave them the dirtiest and
toughest jobs to do. They used the
Hebrews as slaves, making them dig
clay, shape bricks and labour in the
fields all day, and always in conditions
of great hardship.

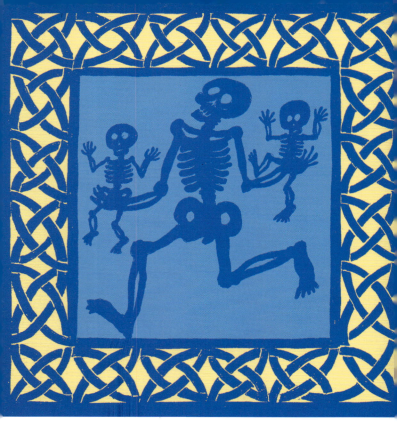

Then the Pharaoh spoke to the Hebrew
midwives, women who helped mothers
to have their babies.
"When the women give birth, kill the
boy babies, but let the girl babies live."
But the midwives believed in God and

did not obey the Pharaoh, and allowed
the boys to live. The Pharaoh said to
the midwives, "Why are you letting the
boys live?" They told him, "Hebrew
women give birth easily and they have
their babies before we can get there."

God rewarded the midwives by giving them children of their own. And so the Hebrews went on and on increasing.

Then the Pharaoh gave this command
to all his people: "Take every newborn
Hebrew boy and throw him in the River
Nile. Let the girls live."

The Hebrews were filled with dismay
and despair. One woman, married to
a man descended from Joseph's family,
gave birth to a beautiful, strong boy.
She could not bear him to be killed,
so she kept him hidden for three months.

But the time came
when she could no
longer hide her baby.
She had to find
another way of
keeping him alive.

The mother decided that she would
leave her baby in the River Nile and
trust in God to look after him.
She made a basket out of reeds, and
covered it with tar to keep the water
out. Then she placed the baby boy
inside the basket.

She put the basket among the tall grasses and bulrushes at the river's edge, and asked her daughter to watch from a little distance away to see what would happen.

After a while, the girl saw the Pharaoh's daughter come down to the river to bathe, while her servants walked along the river bank.

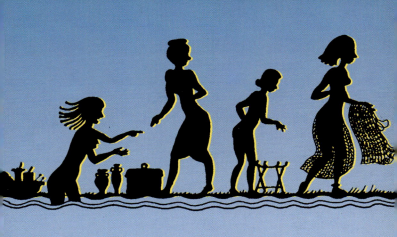

The princess caught sight of the floating basket, and asked one of her servants to fetch it.

The princess opened the basket and saw the baby boy inside. He was crying and she felt sorry for him.

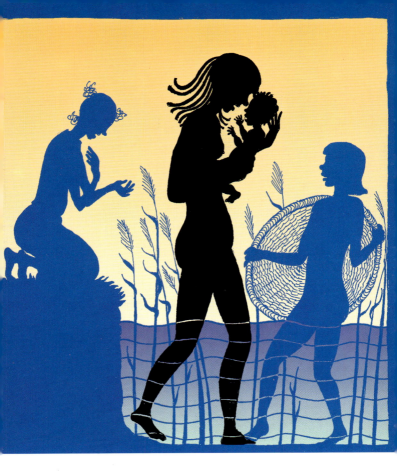

"This must be a Hebrew boy," she said.
Then the baby's sister asked the princess,
"Shall I go and find a Hebrew woman
to take care of the baby?"

The princess agreed to the plan.
The girl then went away and brought
back the baby's own mother.
The princess said to the woman,
"Here, take this baby. Feed and rear him
for me, and I will pay you well."

So the mother took the baby, her own
baby, and fed him and looked after him.
Now she could bring him up in peace!

Later, when the child was older, the woman took him back to the Pharaoh's daughter. The princess loved the boy and now adopted him as her own son.

The princess named the boy Moses.
This name sounds like the Hebrew for
take out.
"After all," she said to herself, "I did
take him out of the water."

And this is how it was that Moses came to grow up at the court of the Pharaoh of Egypt.

Moses was educated like a prince: he
learned to read and write hieroglyphics,
and he was shown the art and wisdom
of Egyptian culture.

Best Bible Stories

The stories in this collection introduce children to characters and themes that they will meet again and again in art, music and literature, and in everyday language. People have found spiritual insights in the stories for centuries.

Our *Best Bible Stories* are retold close to the original scriptures, after comparing several of the most respected translations, including *The Good News Bible* (1994), *The New English Bible* (1970), *The New Jerusalem Bible* (1990) and *The Revised Standard Version* (1973).

The aim of this series is to make the stories more accessible and attractive to children, using clear language without stylistic effects or old-fashioned expressions. Occasionally, and to avoid repetition, narrative has been simplified. Long genealogies have been cut out. The only additions are brief explanations of key ideas – what a prophet is, why sacrifices are significant – and these are built into the text.

Jacqueline Vallon, who devised this series, is editor of religious books for children at Gallimard Jeunesse, in France. She also has experience as a teacher of literature and French, and as a journalist specialising in world religions.

Maurice Pommier used to be a sorter with the French postal service. He taught himself to draw and has always created stories with pictures for children. But it was only when a friend insisted he show his work to a well-known Paris publisher that he embarked on his second career, as an illustrator creating and contributing to a wide variety of books for children and adults. Seen here in a self-portrait with a long, Biblical beard, he likes illustrating Bible stories because he feels that they are timeless and true.

MOONLIGHT PUBLISHING

*PUBLISHERS OF MULTICULTURAL BOOKS INTRODUCING
CHILDREN TO THE RELIGIONS OF THE WORLD*

TALES OF HEAVEN AND EARTH